Chinese Blue

Chinese Blue

poems

Weyman Chan

Talonbooks

Talonbooks
P.O. Box 2076, Vancouver, British Columbia, Canada v6b 3s3
www.talonbooks.com

Typeset in Palatino and printed and bound in Canada.
Printed on 50% post-consumer recycled paper.
Cover illustration by David Blackwell.
Typeset & cover design by Typesmith.

First printing: 2012

The publisher gratefully acknowledges the financial support of the Canada
Council for the Arts, the Government of Canada through the Canada Book
Fund and the Province of British Columbia through the British Columbia Arts
Council and the Book Publishing Tax Credit for our publishing activities.

The author wishes to thank the Alberta Foundation for the Arts for a grant
that greatly assisted in the writing of this work.

LIBRARY AND ARCHIVES CANADA CATALOGUING IN PUBLICATION

Chan, Weyman
    Chinese blue / Weyman Chan.

Poems.
ISBN 978-0-88922-681-4
    I. Title.

PS8555.H39246C45 2012   c811'.6   C2011-908720-0

Canada Council   Conseil des arts
for the Arts   du Canada

BRITISH COLUMBIA
ARTS COUNCIL
An agency of the Province of British Columbia

Alberta
Foundation
for the Arts

for
community

❖

Contents

Five

Six

Seven

1974

ozone

bowl cut, weak eyes

nothing goes by without being
spoken

dust

I forgot

men in black

it's all for you, baby

One

1974

I swallowed a penny
not convinced that God was
in fact (everything) watching

in the currency of 1308
as decreed by Pope Clement V
a penny was worth an entire year's sins

it bought a Dubble Bubble
five of them got you a Pep Chew
or Fanta grape for fifteen

laying one down on the rails
squished a child's sightline
through incoming freight and foundry

to mint it new
like a cloud over the barn
points its weather vane

over mystified spirits
choosing alchemy
over heads or tails

while branches flip
out of hanging necessity
clean and syllabic as

sidewalk chalk tallies odds
in future light
penny wise or pound foolish

can hang strange fruit
ripened by deniers
whose plain optimism

in my lifetime mercy horrifies.
Moonie weddings
and Krishna bells

gain a penny for *my* thoughts
in case theirs vanish
pot growers and Patty Hearst

saved the world or
thought they might earn for the poor
a place in that grove

Heidegger and Hesse
dilate the self to know so little
why the "Do not disturb"

click in the pocket is
more often than not lint
though the magpie

knows a shiny thing or two
about slow roadkill
one by one adds to the count

now is the measure of waste
"I'm not" is always
more than "I am"

> *the will to pray*
> *a soft-slippered earth spirit*

ozone

clouds never were the brave defence
we hoped for
white arctic light made a poor firewall
though it riddled
the back of my head with rainbows

more than what protects us
I trust the defect
that leaves big shady holes in good sense

is there a link to thermohaline
conveyors and serotonin where
over the course of their
dark skin wars
hair colour and eye slant seemed to matter less

now I find myself trading the reaper's staff
for the child's skipping rope
maybe better or worse off

      but what have
such outcomes earned me in place
of perpetual worry

are random acts of continuation
searching for politeness
in the face of famine
where it might all turn pretty again

Supposing that gentler times arrive and
downtown elms wave their sap smell
over this rage of four cleavers
brawling out the back door of W.K. Chop Suey
in 1970 chasing a bunch of gweilo
who didn't pay for their sumptuous parfaits

the logograph for mother + child *means* good
Dad being one of those skinny nimble chefs bearing down

from junked
porch spun
on a tree-swing I turn to Dickie Dee

examine dice to divine its wish
around the corner it becomes its own weather
one chef hangs back while the rest surround
this court of oaths
I have no words for
whose musical Eu-nek ma-ga hai
is a bright bird aria
signifying spring

bowl cut, weak eyes

That year under the flowers
an electric wand is earthed
and blind tribute leaks juicily
from dirt to hook   we never get there. Separation
of corruption from dirt is a power left to worms,
small, squished, dispensable.

For years I've been tacked to your saliva grid
of approvals. Careful to approach. Leaving
always with one foot gnawed.
In dirt you have it easy, sliding out like there was
a hole to escape from all along like
radio signals in deep space dial out
hidden worlds. Yours I found
in an original photo.
Chicago, 1964, it said on the back. Whoever
she is grins through shades feted by undue sentiment.
Your jazz antidote a cheap tie clip.
Will you/I disappear? Come on, don't be

afraid of that last fond kiss I'll be five or six,
your ghost-white cook's uniform smelling
of boiled bipolar spinach
before I recognized you
as candles sufficed to calm us in the power outage.

Enough of the geeky expectations—it was a pleasure
not to go fishing.
A habit set apart.
You've got new teeth now while I've become falsely delicate.

will cursory
multiple readings of him
end the same

nothing goes by without being spoken

I really wish I could make it dirty
like Frank O'Hara did
taking his MoMA loafers to the roach
I strike the page through his eyes he
blows the hinges off its wings

spent proteins barrel
through Freon blouses at some edgy thing to say
to painters and assertive moms who'd
imbibe the finer points of
his scuzzy parrying over Chopin—

for if sound is grammar
revolving its parasol against carbon credits,
if Mort Feldman's Victrola pimps out
cubist expenditures for its own sake,
then, Frank, aren't you the

toast of aesthetes gushing
I'm the centre of everything
while my orphan's mask slips?
Your clink too cool to be morose,
oh, Frank, I love you, please get up

*I've observed
how writers hope to transcribe
then transcend an idea with
numerous hedgings that may or may not
be intended*

dust

the cloud asks not
　　not
　　　how may the
　　　　Arab Spring back the light that burns
　　　　　　　　　　each desire to please
lightning that's trapped from finding its ground
　　　　　by
　　　　　　contracting friction of air
　　　　　　　　　　embeds
the body's paper
　　　discontent
　　　　　　　　　　　ferment
　　　that the goddess of democracy tore
　　　　　　　　　　one snappy flash makes peace with
pavilions and peaches
　　　　　　fire in heaven you'd think that the big voice is order but
　　　　　　　expectation convenes judgment

　　　sweat waterboards my forehead
　　　　a hundred pages could fall to cumulus
　　　　while your soft pink hourglass lips

　　　reach a few hidden sparrows
　　　　who are the described
　　　　not the despaired

I forgot

Same bird or different bird
Different branch or same branch
Home has landed her everywhere
But my home is this one place.

It stays with me when I'm least attached.
From far away I became a rough believer
Comparing myself to the diminished
Least-ranked sparrow

Who slips across this huge quiet
To be herself with me   I breathe her off.
Bird time is so quick it misses
The same light snow that tempers it.

Speakeasy billowese   with flared stops
Scaled off into dusk that
With the years settled me in its past
Before I knew there were wings

Stalled between safe zones.
Now the falling note compares itself
To breezes on a backyard flower
That rose to the way I wandered.

random acts
of continuation
a chance
to start over

men in black

agency—what's that
    a blueprint for action
    tweed Visine metro
    document evid—   *hhhh*
    no witness no smoking shoe
    so who do they work for
secrecy—what's that

2

rain scratches turntable grey
my oilcloth hood soldered
fixated Asperger's lunch-steps
to avoid puddles

      magpies and suits
      steal a shine

      birds feel beneath their feet
      on slouched back Wall Street

don't dive in   cellphone dust can be vacuumed
and voice-recognized but who
cares to listen
well you can't, and with it all the world's
refresh rates mass
cloud data farmed by query. Take from me

3

* my aerial connotation on caring
* as a tiger on a paper ledger shoves its numbers down
  pneumatically

am I tool enough for
our polar-melt-for-slippers deal
industry fuming my already-parched guts with
sleeper cells—who knew?

(my mind when I'm being literal
begs not to become too fixed
then self-effaces and I can't remember
the figurative leap that delivered it)

4

mother to a lot of things, orbiting pheromones in Gaga mouth
trounce up the avenue of marine paint recombinant clapboard—
St. Andrews By-the-Sea, gabled
row house selling knitted mermaids
fresh scallops next door
you knew growing up here that the cannons on the wharf
were as humane today as whale-watching, days
so quiet the rain's recession seemed a controlled wait
to say, in topography or elegy, who you are
felt through clicky knees, domestic comprehension of tides, thick-
chimed and hoisted grey
Passamaquoddy grey

it finds bicycling radioactive
it reduces chance
- to administrative chains of custody sitting bright-eyed
  at the end of *Star Trek*
- butterflies' flipped dice
  pin down our imagining

5

brackish air over lithic
years slurred underfoot
reading the land is like going over Hebrew without the vowels'
opaque concretions to sound the marsh palate, the inlet's tongue

fog's long soft *o*
sits shearwater grey over each
rock node consonant *s*
for seashore   document (fresh scallops)
before you
liquidate
disappear but our retinas still glow cyanide
seen for miles at low tide

6

that's him
    smashed in
    lexical know-it-all
    swings the body around if
    betrayal shortens the tail
    to sharpen the teeth
he's our guy

dis-allusioned bean-counter   Crave cupcake
partaker of tightly cut atmospheres

Sarah drives on past the post office to meet us.
We stay over, she plays *Figaro* on her Amphion gramophone.
Tools who feed the groove must
take on the master's voice
I tell her that the pocket-smallness of Bocabec
Cove seems to be watching us or at least
the outdoor dicta of infrequent traffic
and birds feeling through their feet for worms
are signals by which all treachery and alibi
have burned the ends of each sacred hour
telling me I'm not tired yet   but
I'm on Calgary time. Her uprooting from kids and grandkids
almost in relief now that we're three hours ahead of that life.
We'll talk deep into the night

those in black are
alone   source code dependent
on expedience and influence
divided by

7

nails to pick apart a face that lonely beds matriculate   poor
enough to convince me that everything I don't want is wanted

small bombs in me aren't new
they'll explode unnoticed or
those who follow the rapture index will
hurl through my pressed suit looking for someone
porous enough for their
good equivocation and suppurating use

while black expectation sails through his feet

*so she gets into the cab same time I do then puts this perfect hand on my lap
and for the next ten minutes we watch helicopter footage where as soon as the
tsunami starts overtaking the tiny moving dots the camera turns away, my
lap wishing we'd started out smoking and far apart, too alive to hold*

8

she approaches I
    am not the death
    denier who parts the
    sea analogue that
    exuberance mutilates
    Seurat loved cigars
sensing our amusement

    to scratch, rub, write or insist
    how the speaking subject and the history of science
    are flawed recordings
    people distance tumbling

cannons on the wharf
an ornament's deterrent

    takes out his notepad puts it away
    first word *equivalence*—last word *continuity*—
    grant him perplexity to believe that
    the missing heart never was
    and the speakeasy on Tenth's hidden menu on
    Hunan pulled-pork sliders

is everything
I mean to say

it's all for you, baby

for D.C.

maybe it's sundown for us
in the chrome of our Coupe de Ville
wiped out on gangplanked roofies and
you with your Stockholm Syndrome weren't the one to leave
Maggie and Wayne who kept sunshine in bottles at
the tuna-slurping commune in White Rock

last I'd heard they were living righteously
weaning themselves off Bobby (a.k.a. Bunnyboiler) and
swimming with tulips   Who knew
you were only after the strawberry air
freshener in my saddlebag? Or, stay together—occasionally
to grow up, silly-assed dim-wit
jackalope on the mantel your
third wheel jealously walloping when daisy chain
used to mean daisy chain

"Nights in White Satin" still binding us to its background.
Sunset Drive-In double header, *Jeremiah Johnson*
followed by *Enter the Dragon*—and you did,
my son's GI Joes on cinder-block shelving,
Planet of the Apes action set
in its own carrying case. Playing *Pong*
to Tangerine Dream. You were
his everything for a while.
Now lumped in with mind-melds and lightsabers.

At Yesterdays in Westwood the napkin fell on you.
Today's the library dining room of the Fairmont Algonquin.
In walks Joe Clark with his grandkids. We talk.
You tell him you make a living off of poetry. *I wish.*
You speak too loud and, by way of acquaintance,
about Yma Sumac? How apt—
five-octave romance
or jungle calls too shrill to lunch with?
Shut up and enjoy your bisque.
That's what you pay for, laughs Joe.
One of us should go first. Not the Pope,
and you'd know him too, wouldn't you? Still
down on frivolous advances.

❖

Alberta blues

current infrastructure

Two

tonight
the silkworms
spin us free

❖

Alberta blues

Oil on reserve
and one out of seven jobs that our
pond life will draw from the ground
in this charmed slurrying

chickadee-dee-dee
on a diamond-toothed augur
is spirit appeased by pipe
smoke now carefully worded

in civic treaties that ad
hoc serious feathers for cash
looking down from the weather vane
that points to roadkill

aren't we magnifyingly brilliant
to reach inside this desert's
old green self? If the boy was a boy
drawing himself in ruts of sidewalk chalk—

pigs   paladins   Jabberwocks
to leave his wings of tar behind
deposing the lord of scarecrows
to become me—then he succeeded

every sulphide oracle fume
shaking hands with fields
of mill rates and royalties
while city gaps part the grass

and teepee rings
meet the disappeared   our tick
boom logic will bounce
any twig to flip its shiny bird

                                        curved roofs
                                are for looking up

current infrastructure

safe enclosure

Fevers and sweet nothings. Put Occam's Razor to a xylophone.
The bars between are tutelary.

Ryanne says that my name tastes like chocolate bananas.
But a bit of synesthesia never cut up anyone.
Persistent sightings of Kurt Cobain on cruise ships will build
consensus that one's showy pant cuffs won't
normally typify.
Learn to separate ideas from wounds.

I'm late meeting the Two Small Men with Big Hearts.
They're moving out Dad's bed-furniture again, after cigarettes, duelling
walkers, dentures, Gravol and spit-up have
straightways and right-of-ways clogging Deerfoot with
my Tim Hortons such that
the very tediosities nucleating inside aren't any better at
expediting the A plus B gets you to see
fewer dilemmas to the ongoing rubric of getting old.

Love hurts to go the wrong way
now that I'm closed to everyone who has anything to do with
who's in charge

fraudulent causes

Perfect advertising stole you. Perfect advertising.pdf.exe
shrank the file that gave a shit.

Maybe that's why I need to distance myself from logical structures,
mumbles O'Hara. Frisco has Ginsberg
while Pollock has himself—substantiating his frontal goo.
Doodled all over my back like I was his.
What a hangover. What a goofy top he'd make, vintage light
all over me like a bound fresco. Or Larry R.,
sloshing his wrists open, 'cause he'd hunt like I do for black trophies,
if it weren't for his eroticization of the oppressor.
Jane knows he paints nudes of me just to keep her away.
I say, Jack! Stop rubbing yourself like a nickel.
He says, Christ, Frank. Go to the front desk
and pound away like you're typing index cards.
Any strained contents—suitcase, brain—leaves prints.
No one should have aneurysms
just to feel good. Well that's me, Jack.
Gonna meet my maker with Maria Callas soaring.
Gonna roll Him under my Rorschach dune buggy

penal correspondence

getting kicked out of a senior's home for smoking makes sense
they don't mention water poured on carpeting
single-handedly he pushes back his desert
great spotted mildew oases sprout from baseboards
he always complained of parched sinuses versus childhood, whistling
his pet oriole down from her lonely solstice. Magpies in Calgary don't
sing like his did, though they do remind him of those grey swoops
off the fields—Cantonese. Toisan. Hakka. Shouted over squat and
seed, swear and harvest, he wants to mint himself a future he can see,
though now it easily blacks out a bingo card. Shouting helped get him
here, I could track and even take back my inherited likes and dislikes
just listening to him—whose fault is that?—then lose my way

one almost needs an obstacle to accessorize
for which I phoned in sick saying I have anal glaucoma
what the hell is that she says, her pursiness rowing on air
that means I can't see my ass coming into work today
what would barfly Bukowski say
about limpness that keeps performing,
a few bird strands of cursory nest
can unravel any time   who knew
all the crackerjack swag and bouffant this city
swings from alphabets,
dim-lit backroom ball-and-chain image consultants
dolled up, chased and then chaste
is, at the end of it, a month of Sundays left to leave some trace

each sign a kind of want for what's not wanted
which succeeds in getting you off the streets
then you trip on an Aspirin
at Shinjuku Station and get sucked under   oops

then holding court you describe yourself in
archetype with the morning prune juice and static shuffleboard
all the ladies here think you cute indeed
maybe an epistemology of consequence
has me on the run
Navajo idea that *mind* isn't
one's own possession it's
out there   all encompassing   therefore
you're mine

could torment by association be more
tenuous when such
deputations don't help
the dumb-winged acrobat on my finger
I've killed just to let luck and smooth sailing
be an adequate description for it? *It*
being those who commit relevance to conformity of *love*.
Goldfinger showed how skin breathes
or else you die
so go ahead   touch me
tell me what you feel
there's no proof of pain

watering bok choy from a garden hose

born of earth taken
in warm rain
his undershirt always white and cool—now resting
under mythical lilacs
back to the very field
where he sold his brother
if the flood-stripped sway of a runaway father rose and ran off
with the swish of a carp's tail
and evening's swampy pearl
was itself too late for the lotus to get up and scream
well there may be horns of Africa seen in a pair of cloud-bound feet
in ever-widening V-necks, she's
from the night sky and he's hard done by

no half-stopped clear
flute-on-buffalo *cheng-ku*
the last peak
incomprehensible

lightning below the uplands

I work on the floor of secretaries
they are over the moon with clinical reporting's interruptus
of photocopiers and Wite-Out
that's not to say
that the missing pathologists I work for on that other floor
aren't any particular drag on air as someone
else planting my floor with ventriloquists may
sound verbose alarms when a report on clogged canaliculi goes AWOL
I channel my construct-system denial
taking micrographs of metastases under
periscopes of green lantern light
the dark's clipped centromeres copying themselves to death

Kate and Wills didn't see that when they waved from the Hyatt
kitty-corner to Arts Central
so nothing was reported
I mean who knew life was free to overlook
you'd get off on some laugh track this northern arctic psychodrama
springs on the royal we
or is this your free but lonely
(*frei aber einsam*) talking—
and the Twitterverse wants what?

No, it's better to work, said the boy who served Frank his morning
bourbon and OJ before he got his poems dirty …
as maidens braid the manes of their mares
might be one way to start a good day with no roof on it
before those dealing suits cut your thread

seasonal hobos
told to load up on strawberries and then leave

father as beekeeper

the zzzzzz of death is jangling enough Venn puddings to split
horoscopes with the usual pointless aloneness conflating the I of self
and other, one such evening Dad, aged fifteen, looked south and
found him, his father, half-dead among the bean rows after pissing
away the landowner's advance on women in Whampoa or Hoi Seng,
no one knew, but now a row of trellised sunflowers and hollyhocks at
his first home in Regal Terrace greets the first peaceful glance south in
a long while

trellis

Start off with some levity at the mouth of self-interest and think,
Marilyn. Whose neon pop chanteuse preened over those transparency
overlays of skin-muscle-skeleton-circulation in *World Book Encyclopedia*.
Flip through them fast enough and your meat and nerves will blur self
and document, like that "Printer's ink is the greater explosive" sign
above the stairs to the poetry room at City Lights Bookstore only refers
to the wish that makes you buy into the buried syntax of bookstores.
You don't know me, but I've always been here.
I've always read over your shoulder like an unwanted afterlife.
Afterlife, my foot. We're one sneeze away from a bright flash that ends
in silence.
Words work as advertised. So do circumcision, paramedics and Malbec.
Aspen fluff tumbles out the rut of Ohe's vulvic fountain at Prince's
Island while bathing bulrushes high-five petroleum bankers either side
of Lions Gate Bridge.
Water fountain.
Skin that touches off fluorescence around birches
while hyphae rise and shine from ferocious midwife to the same
sun on everyone. Without brightness slipping off to the supreme racket,
your sky wouldn't shouldn't
be blue to the eye.

birds again

it came   it all came from the delicate
non-voiced and birdless nest
next to the clothesline that
seemed to shout to me   here is your summer house
and nothing will exclude you from now on

we hoarded a cluster of thumb-sized potatoes
from Dad and Stepmom's garden
waited until the dead of night so we could toss them in a soup can
and fix candle heat that blackened the bottom until we gave up
excited to crunch down the warm-watered spuds
I won't forget the glow of my brother's my sisters' faces
the high we felt when Dad caught a bird on the fence and left it
trembling inside before going to work   did it appear
many-lived or emptied of heaven
did it match the oriole who summoned him
countless times landing on his shoulder while he barely
a teenager scrounged to feed his mom and three brothers

my sister gives this sparrow a home
sky-blue Lysol lid bedded with toilet tissue
and we watched its breaths of sleep lash the mast—

waiting

frivolous advances found me
the one bed
this one place
contiguous with
shoulder to forelight   service
pressed into your grasp of home
permission for each known
word I look far from
sent out to bring in
who am I to
meaning

search the sky whose
afterbloom divides
the atmosphere in two   we're alien and familiar
from two down to one
fixity no freedom

I'd hoped you'd take
solitude's well-meaning
when I'm with you
for these limits
aren't known
will I be
returned
when I'm not
would any sage
dream without expectation in kind

contact

leaked
informant
astroglider   beware

any nerve
splays its
background noise

eight feelers hunkered down on my sternum she
spins ownership over
politicos

I have
no
unguent to offer

sprockets blur
the floating road spray self
assembles its protein swing

why do I appear to
be happening
just as I stop and think about it

where if not here will she court my concupiscence?
could I swing on handsprings
white flags

Riopelled over blinks and blunders that
got me behind
to get me here

little eye
save my stiff
puppet fluids

for climbing
who knew
your art could crush me between the word and the thing

his apple pies used bacon fat,
not shortening

intermission at the gallery opening

like

still life

stud fever, Brylcreem, glasses
—a portrait viewed through
regression analysis

Sedona

Three

with one serene breath
"heart like dead ash"
"a frame like withered wood"
Hu Tzu
withdrew

his apple pies used bacon fat, not shortening

deep-sea radio tomography may be
riding dolphins into the ground right now

July fireworks flood the poles for less muggy hammocks
not to be confused with ruptured capillaries kayaking
over bled animalcules in the back
of my head, zinging exponentially—

now's not the time for this Fellini chorus
tripping the ionosphere with its whiskers
when our neighbour's grey tabby tries to untuft
my sister who measures a saucepan full of our boys' acrid pee
that she pours from the vinegar jug I bring out of the bathroom

from the green rain barrel
my sister adds three saucepans of water to the urine
and lugs the tin pail over to the snow peas
the flies smell it too   so does Tiger
whose swishing tail churns flourishing spinach rows

our makeshift night soil drifts like a rotary
blade across picket and lilac to our Dutch neighbours
in colours that cannibalize their straitlaced
splotches like a Cretaceous fern or a late Cézanne
makes peace between harsh primaries
I grew fond of their shouts and slammed doors and
drunken arguments snouting out our handmade vegetable pee

while my sister grimaced through her duties to the patch
to drag Tiger through the tall grass with fish guts
tied to a string   no deceit

just playfulness and reward accompanied Tiger's
pouncing meow from gap-toothed swill
to our gangster-sized table scraps

if mornings could remain a comfort and a gift
that by late afternoon would
land us in the familial maw
of a long bright concentric dressing down from the west

❖

intermission at the gallery opening

The beauty of its automation means that
I don't need to flush, touch water taps or soap pump
or even assume the tired

labour of a cement-mixing slave who in oppressed times
built the cistern that held the keys to this
agency that flowed and fountained like a curve in the *logos*

if good civic manners slip there's always Bauhaus
efficiency remaining—long halls
and Kafkaesque echoes
someone says fuck off and the mirror says pardon me, sir

that tile pours continuous to the sidewalk upon which
you're happily hooked on whatever etched its soundproofing
so you become that other space

give in to cleaning yourself and blessing the skylights
hot air and drain changes which sanitize the blood
and dirt on you as if

cradling its hygiene across the hollows
to meet up with you (system without value)
the ambience owes you an apology
a mere function of that intended intent

parting your citron-scented towelette

like

Me from *you* is one more
oven-haired grind when you stir a few drops of morphine
into your morning cup. Friends at King Ying restaurant
take you in every night.
Last year you buried your wife,
warm headstones and plastic roses blessing the many
in as few visiting hours as possible
for those fighting to stay on.

Easy to laugh. Easy to cry.
At least your sister-in-law let us
get our heads stuck in her banister in Victoria.
Birds have it easy, twittering ghosts of tree interments
they dart and pull worms like fat gossip,
no one's grounded in despair, no one's
serrated from the dead. A tree unclasps
what's fleeting under its branches.
Things move off their face, and today I'm
moving in fear of doing nothing.
Clamouring against my silence.

A window is just a window composing
clarity—diehard tricycle jousts
you had to mediate along the elms on Ninth
when you wouldn't play after setting up
badminton net over unmown grass. You watched for a bit,
hero to unredeemed quiet inseparable from yourself, cigarettes
enlarged like nudes ascending
the smoke of thirty thousand shimmies,
caught in the first pink buds of lust,
then sudden old age,
recognizing one inside the other.

You're at a crossover point believing that and
lighting your swagger once and for all.
You see this would've also pleased your dad.

There you go—pleasing your dead again.
Like has nothing to do with it.
Think of a bridge and see what comes.

still life

in the bunker slides a periodic table
of appetite   breath   sound
held apart by their element

the walls stare
the cells hold their hourly water
like unbreakable beakers

Magda Goebbels before she sent
her six kids one by one to *Tiefland* on the last
day

must've seemed joyous or relieved
when it had been decided
that it almost was to be—

Reich matriarch with Bette Davis eyes
she had to keep silly stenographer Eva
in line   everyone knew who
wore the pants

to build a mercy seat out of
a field of cornflowers and
boxcars that chuffed
all night to get it done

❖

stud fever, Brylcreem, glasses—a portrait viewed through regression analysis

Don't be your medium. Don't identify with yourself. Just as a mirror can only get up as close as you can. Rock gardens are themselves. Water too. They only mix at points of contact so nothing gains supremacy. Integers attenuate. At the end of all wisdom, a mystic has nothing to show for it except a few adjectives. Scrofulous uploads orbit a second sun on our city, staring dispassionately from place settings of supernumerary items. Foundries of cutlery de-cloak. Please go back to your room with its lace and paper flowers.

first session

include the entrapments
integers build
one parent dies of cancer
one goes off his rocker
then two children
are put in row-on-row cribs
the light of its auditorium
spare and industrial
we exchange a blue toy piano
between the bars
my sister and I
are two and four years old
there are other echoes fast
memories of two more
one brother one sister
they don't appear and we're
forgetting to ask
their names among the faceless
dreads   end-on-end cribs
two years old no grown-up to lift me out

being here is like being stuck between causes, as far as one is drawn
to pistol size on the shooting range like there's some willing target
to my crazed cartoon backscatter. Too late getting through the men's
room door as I'm told I'm insensitive. Now I'm off into the big wide
world to find me a bride. Nose hairs, teeth and shoes. To consistently
buff according to template may present more defined refinements to
summer torso as breeding success with sequelae will favour surly and
smouldering types

don't kiss don't tell

a private grief asking
a place for zero to have
its vacant sign on
for the sake of its box of colours
this side of the garage
he stands beneath a tree staring
past the bees at a loss he can't define
maybe there's subservience in the call
of his name in English
the foster parents teach him cows in the barn
make milk
his first stomach ache
sun goes down fast him out-staring the tummy pain
in tree shade high summer
a mom without

in the meantime sports offer tribe fulfillment strength being the
prime stag rack to parachute over enemy lines risking the small
nothingness Mother Courage would to prime bullshit for stealing
chickens leaving that nipple's flash of toothpaste might also give
me the world if I lived through war and now leak at slow yoga and
shuffleboard while diaper-padded as far as one dread could wreck an
entire tournament—did buying in mean that the *i* before *e* elasticity
would jinx the last crack of my wit to make them say at the cutthroat
Scrabblethon table—*he's cheating?*

second session

the part about
loss of Chineseness
is about whose peril
compels the latest worry
so he dreamed of an identity
not of mah-jong grocers
florists or dim sum cart pushers
but of masked men
the red of Iron Man
the gold blue of Dr. Fate
their powers will bail you out
like the blood of children
pretend they can
power envomitous plasmas from their spandexed arms
such padded strength
a boy's lost uniform

our defences fortify the dead as if six directions pulled together in one collective packing-up of troubles in old kit bags could razz any boys' adventure better than this stitch of a difference—the moment of entrapment—when you sit up in your dark cot and see murder behind the barrel and still find a way to salute the peace in your firmly inherited jaw. One marvels at numerous surveillance antennae from the footnotes up (past street-level tacticians pawning a future with no gods to voice a man's body nation) so why not elect this parity with death through a child's leap from brother to hood to grave? I've learned to wrap my shadow around me

today's will

bring cold feet
and dulcet-toned
yen for lucky
leaps in
commune donkey-sharing
1949 and 1989
we must all think alike
charging the bullet
cost of each revision
your rose-coloured
default

hockey and football and golf stats aside, the history of active
deterrence may not be linked except randomly to any fostering of
mineral rights or people's rights, yet here we are with our swing and
sporty flak jacket while marching bands stop and someone plays taps
to Mother Armistice yet again. Equal parts love and phosphorus, I
smell of winning in our foreseeable scrum which will come, randomly
I would opine, if you stand back a ways and simply let the dots
connect themselves to the great ball and mitt in the sky that will teach
him as I was once taught, never throw one except in self-defence, but
if he's hit below the belt—well then, pity the opponent

third session

to build an implosive over
mass potting soils
a square lake doubles the sun's mind
over Khmer roots
at Angkor
the jungle panjandrum's
blood coursing appliqué
best serves his
rapid-beating aftertaste
breasts carved in relief
flood the hall of mirrors

I don't care to go into this don't-ask-don't-tell watermelon's bodily functions when no one gives a shit. But the mock of our desires often needs a hive to kick or a set of teeth to wear down—yes sir no sir—when our goose step starts to feel like walking casual. There's a kind of tough-all-over the Flames versus Canucks tonight. Oilers got lazy. Pressure toward ever-faster chariots is about as handsome as the keel of a Whiskey-class submarine. Deep killers glide best in mission statements. You're a champ not a chump, so let your boots do the talking.

Sedona

The sun's a broken watch
says this puritan ethos of desert
so loved by adobe night birds.
Vicodin vicodin vicodin.

Turquoise on my sternum
a garnet he calls ruby
will be the heart that softens.
Red rock screws the mare out of oats.

Four gated beings stick to a candle
in that window shop whose
druid bible rewrote the potion
on chakras, yoni bells and fire.

Hot tub baristas and facial Adonises
cob-pipe it down from Bell Rock
to some other red-bottomed stupa
certain to assume the mission creep

you pray for but don't vortex.
Flabby-lipped spirit-seller,
Glinda of lifted smiles,
declare your temple restored.

joys of the season

me instead of you

patternicity of yowling cats

sweeter than unbaptized hair

late-night sports commentary

the colour yellow

Four

the tree
fell
on
me
what did it learn

joys of the season

That flavour of ice cream
is called Cotton Candy Circus.
I walk by the Marble Slab forgetting what's
meant in a name
after all it is Christmas Eve—packed
malls and snowpack that's a tune outside
lumbering sleigh bells or snow mangers
depending on who you talk to

well the Charlie Brown tree I dragged inside
got mud and needles on my kids' feet
there were marshmallow experiments
done to three year olds who anticipated
but deferred the thing they liked and so became wiser
and Brenda Lee on mall speaker
followed by "Attention, shoppers"
—it's all staged radio folksiness
fending off mixed mayhem

while Sally Ann jinglers jingle on.
Faint blue star over her hem
swishing by. The sky's also rushing
in with the dark, weightless X of mass
that wants to quicken our red-suited figures of now—

but where is the joy of now?

Awaken. Back to the eyelids of children
and a clear tune outside

guessing wintergreen or the flying
smell of juniper
she helped her son into his tiny coat then drew down

the hood and pulled the strings tight until
he was all halo-wide eyes and cheeky anticip—

all it takes is
one memory and
you're stunned by Joplin's "Piece of My Heart"
bellicose and harrumphing, speed-shopping end over sock.
God knows, some photos
need touching up.
Sleep and gratitude will and do
get you through it.

But a parent holding a child
near? We recognize it,
tapered carousel and wingless arrival
with warm blankey and milk moustache—
Look.
Tomorrow's wrapped in gold.
Tomorrow will open its trees
as easily as tonight
packs them as gifts.

resist

who I was
to what I saw

me instead of you

figures   doesn't it   lord
              of December
         Stepmom throwing around the
        tree gifts   shouting   the presents! sabotage!
  the wish of death upon our household!
    black curse she throws them
   against the wall while I shout
 shrieking in my pajamas Dad
               who tells her to shut up she won't
     so kapow! he hits her retreats to his
    evening shift she calls
       the police they come look
      at her she sits there sobbing in Chinese
            I caress the orange tree leaves the leaves of
ornamental mimosa that go limp
     watch them turn their fronds down when you touch come and look
       where's your dad? I tell them
                they go
     think swallow think cake
         and tree decorating at least
  the tree lights up at night I would've liked a real one
     but that hadn't happened since 1968

        everyone's a comedian
         who can tell kids anything
         they'll want to believe in
     come drink cow-brain soup! he
         gets us out of bed at 2 a.m.
              the bowls are murky brains afloat
         to fit the porcelain spoon
           choking down maybe

we can slip it down our pants

but my brother gets caught gets the blue bat

come on   you have to

swallow can't go to bed till   s   bitter

roots   *ouwwwwhhh*

with a pair of tongs

simply
not saying
persists
toward

❖

patternicity of yowling cats

First I saw the Virgin's buns
on a crumpet thinly spread with Marmite

next day Liz Taylor was passing overhead while
I was in the Second Cup chewing
through a stone-ground bran muffin that humped my dish like a
cinnamon buffalo

"Walking on Sunshine" was blaring on the radio
and I knew Liz Taylor was finally dead
while the tomcat's barbed meat was busier than my uncle's blind
pocket knife whittling through days of espresso decaf
in a war without heroic advantage
although the itch and the scratch of it
don't seem to be working for me
Frank, you keep calling me prissy in your church basement wearing
Marilyn Manson kill-frill as if
the world should cheer fakers like me slinking and slunkering down
flights of stairs for the endless party flotation effect
I could pop them out of my centrifuge and have the Lord too
in my heart that is

should the Lord's shortbread taste like anybody else's
did He have a double set of eyelashes too?
I'm hoping for the sake of eternally cycling karmas that it does and
yes

Marx said the Lord has
nothing to do with it

well okay then I'll want Groucho to at least commandeer the
Sistine nudes tumbling endlessly in my tea leaves
like Krusty the Clown
channelling De Niro's serious analysis
that's all liquid cat
with hyacinth to mother

Personal and cultural
duplicity

getting you down?

sweeter than unbaptized hair
(after five hours shopping at CrossIron Mills, Balzac)

To be unmovable (say the Taoists)
you've got to be watercolour
you want to soft-focus and penetrate
the ground as if released from it

hope does seem ascetic one day
Byzantine the next
and you always knew that spring
(short on bird gears stringing up the gloom)

was really the sky's brush on you
going through
faster than anyone wearing humility or magic
could to die for you
so the three-legged sunbird of *Huai-Nan Tzu* rises

when stars wink out
"the place without anything" is also bright
its clear polyhedra
twinkling down these arch supports

fast as a night cyclist over black ice
single dying is best
a precise art
nailing each saint to his own light.

My third ear

is my tongue

late-night sports commentary

in view of the orchestral surge at Baja
Carly Simon piped in with Charlie Parker
while Mexican Marxist and Arcade Jew
window washers do flaming Heimlichs from opposing sides
and sheep-cloud ibises hurl their billeted suppers
from McDonald's onto the biographical head
of a bunny rabbit that might be asleep
in this *Where's Waldo* mud in your eye
brought to you by Coca-Cola demise
sliding ever calmly across my insomnia

they know who Dion Phaneuf is here in Baja
Hop Sing at the Ponderosa catches a breeze and rolls one
perhaps he too would've equated *pimple* with *indigenous*
being counted among the ugly and the invisible
who view sloppy seconds as golden opportunities
to breed and photocopy telltale hairs
of the Osama versus Obama long form
on foreigners subject to hoary gossip
since nobody knows to what extent the limits
of freedom must conspire

nobody knows when Stevie will regain
that razed octave her third nostril stole
no one knows when the next new kid
will run amok in the library with his Glock
thinking he's Sarah Palin taking down a moose
while Miss Kitty pulls a mint
six-shooter from her laces
to defend the West from its cross-eyed horse

like a frontier family
gathering history like bales
stored for future broods
can hang out to dry
what any transfiguring of belonging
looks like
not surmising what
he thinks of himself through love of
his children although
the feud with his brother (my father) before it was told
comes out

how Dad chased his brother with a machete for eight hours what do you
think of that asks my uncle's daughter
through fields past mango trees into Hoi Seng
no! not our dad
your dad did the chasing
why would he do that asks
her husband over our reunion dinner and the kicker was
is your dad still crazy
I don't know you need to talk to him I
said my mouth like swatted flies

the colour yellow

congregating red dragonflies
are chased out by the white-and-blue segmented ones

my hands float over the barley's
nodded heads before a great
atomic Trojan with rainbow eyes lands on my knee

I am Wang Wei, said the aleatory thought, obviously trying
to one-up Chuang Tzu. I recognized your stinger, I said.

No longer required. This bug and I have transcended food.

Oh, really, I said to the scaly, cruciform blur. And where would you
like to go with that? My psychoanalyst's best voice.

Wang Wei laughed. Each big breath torqued his segmented torso as
he landed on each of the five grains, rejecting them in turn, as any
immortal should. Quite the show, I said.

*Well, it might be that bugs don't see any gods but themselves, so nothing
would then distinguish them from me. I had to appeal to this one's vanity—
claiming that instinct was a sad, poor widow of free will. It wasn't easy.
These days, the wise are distrusted—even hermits. I had no choice but to
wrestle nature. Yarrow and earth grappled me to the mat. Freedom was in
every breath I took. Death lanced me like the sun's radii. Its light was mine—
as if I'd invented the colour yellow. My wings were—*

The WangWeifly zoomed away, then returned. His six legs clutched a
tatter of cloud. Embedded in the fluff was a corn seed. The corn seed
was built up of layers of names. These layers of names fell from its
cloud as rain.

Let go of the names and you let go of the forms. It loses nothing to be happy,
said Wang Wei to my mind's low-slung appetite, diffuse pigments,
psychic cooties and other proximate loves that bite off more than what
earth chews—

So what, Wang? A fly can still starve when it's dining on clover—

It was then that Wang Wei's tone changed.

*You're still such a sycophant to reason, my boy. The great command is this:
to melt with the sky. In the meantime, you must think of ways of touching
as few beings as possible. Follow the dandelion, which is the bee's garden-
abdomen, and emesis to her queen. Better to be a figment of your own meek
helplessness than the king of mullets, say, or Elvis, who still can't die because
of all that he wants.*

With that last flick of his rah-rah voiceover
plugged to a stingless spine
Wang Wei dissolved

left with this lazy-winged shell of an empty trespass
I turned away
having no misery left in me
to stamp it out

Stephen Hutchings: Sky

temperance swoons admonishment

chemical agency in a Petri dish

art of war

figuration of Frank O'Hara
contemplating my father as
Botero's Smoking Woman

Five

baby baby baby
whooahh
baby baby baby

Stephen Hutchings: Sky

and then it brightened but went
cloud chrome

unyellow   angry   loner
you won the lottery to shut down my blue   slout   slang   if
Varadero rides me out of that serene culmination I plan not to have death

apologize for its   persnickety
way out

corona
dissarona
of the total weight of our futures in the present you'd feel
not heel sprung or escaped through

but hoofing it gently into that good
dark frickathon

we   open   up
without   being   broken
or   maybe   that's   land   wearing
legibly   across   the   crawl   tatter
salient   vocal   heat   to   read   by
not   sure   who   vacations   it   so
now   you   paint   I   splurge   the
overt   slickness   that   the   sun
swept   across   the   ages   where
before   its   mission   voted
continuous   light in our harp glissando we'd flare

                                                 don't say

                         sugar

             your frissons over

        non-raptured

                                    looking back can't tell if

you were a shoulder

                      crossed   dust-off

     should the balls of our tiger lily meet

temperance swoons admonishment

On Sunday Mee Wai had Yang's
balls in her mouth. By Monday
the F-150 wouldn't park.
Girders sardonic with description.
Borders helped her transgress
but they were demarcated by winter.
Starry dunes with blue-lit stern.
Imprint of jean indigo that wore her out
now her textiles forsee
knockoffs as copies of where you wanna be. Travel
portraiture means scanning who goes
obfuscating virtue, what size dress
worked, Blaine and Sally touching on
monkey bars. Flipped Upanishad first year
with Emilio. Microbes on sensitivity
testing, zones of clearing.
Said malingerer ringed efficacy
through exclusion of the senses she
stuffed Emilio. Undressed to deafen light bulbs.
And because laundered love was at best
skeptical, self would fall away like
snowmelt off a roof, all existence pondering her numinous mistakes.
Not her. Call it riveting
blue-jean needles cast out on the soup grey floor.
Long-legged girls of Guangzhou,
why do you doubt Democritus? Call it
one in a billion cherry fruit caught in the rake. Old. Dried.
Either way the senses are awake. Electric
on ordinary. We get away
reading rough drafts, only to be lost in the snow.
Raj Sherman tries to un-bully
manifestos sewn in Nurse Betty's shoes.
The Wild Rose budget on big oil

downs subways for its own personal frack,
who knows if Emilio and Yang ever met.
I never got past page 68.
It's all about tiny details. And knowing
someone's weakness just by looking,
I trade my electron microscope
for plasm-crawlers and
areolas dropped in my mouth. But poems
can't be put down, they crave salt in a ragging rich
Lady Day alto, droozed with aviary port.
Zonky Kirk Miles and swingy Kirk Ramdath.
You branchy sentences at the Auburn,
turn the year different each day.
Sully Stu, Julie, Bill and Cecelia,
Matt, Myra, Eugene and John,
kabuki and plums. Hark my mrozen mouf,
and or of, my body's cloud, to be so encrusted.

chemical agency in a Petri dish

some muscular cigar roller
all-round stickler for laws and due process
with his fine-tipped disposable Eppendorf flourish
is at one with the glass

      a lens is a lens is a lens

prodding cilia to beat absolute zero while
uniting proportions that fail to ignite
on their own

          maybe buffered ions, a Bic lighter and
any off-the-shelf acrosome accelerant
could help me to sit down without hurting
my protractor
         I see him fitting Ivy League pins to horse sperm
Go Harvard!
         and pompoms to hamster oocytes
      now observe how assiduous penetrants push'n'pull

               millions of years between
               first-class dicks will do the prehensile
               while genomecists like her drag their eyeliner
               over douches like me, pilot lit from the night
               before

stab me with your eye
and I'll cool your jets
backbone of sugar
helix of spice
let my hoariness show you how coupled yokes pat down their pokes

look at how cytoplasm guzzles by sol-gel conversion along
lucid limbs (actin-myosin actually)
and self-medicate with knockout sequences and auto-thermocycled
bread warmers I wear for hands

properly sewn on I gallop

the first tropism

by affection (indifference to *Seinfeld*)
and hurt
lying   faffing about
tipped not slouched
shaken not stirred

❖

art of war

1

peace of mind's the one thing
no Rottweiler should in a park
pushing me over just by
saying   do so

yes the Arctic is vulnerable
my piles are flaring majestically
when I was little
I sang strengthless notes and cried thinking
my soreness was backbiters
not pinworms after
reading a book my finger strategy couldn't
sort out whose
unphotographed child I was
in a childhood full of sullied postures

2

I ask myself, how else does
size change feeling at the
viewport of behemoths leering
back at clouds who hum and bark
to a sudden platinum burst

my last-to-be-picked team of marching bands
not yet vented
I threw down pompoms
tried baseball that summer but fell
on my lip effectively
ending the body's competitive arena
storm hazes grew

small-bodied next
to the window behind the radiator that drew heat
from *Mod Squad* commentary and *Room 222*
hobbies not hard-ons, my dear

3

let's be clear about these books of changes
written so cleverly without a father
when platoons and squads engage

one thousand gold pieces per day
will sustain an army and cavalry of one hundred thousand
says *The Art of War*
dreadlocks and battle tactics were already favouring archers
on horseback
while chariots hobbled into Habouba sunsets
in earlier ages most battles were a question of minimal
tactics conquering those with deficient strengths
so military records have conscripted our
vigilant backsides all too pliant from the yoke
how else do sages at watering holes
compose lighthearted verse of eucharistic loss

behead in order to instruct
says the *Ssu-ma Fa*

attack their haste and capitalize on their fears
as opportunity springs at every frontier
avoid and *prepare*
will take the throne

4

camouflage   scrupulous armour
watch
the horse's petunia   feign swiftness and indirection
to strike at their weakness when plum blossoms flee
an enemy rumoured is better than statecraft
upon which to build governance

5

an amoeba turns cannibal
just before it divides asexually
such protoplasmic hunger
on autonomic kill
dwells behind worlds unseen

transistors and nano-ninjas
wall the small of my back
before my eyes are opened
to a breeze of fresh flags won

6

it seems that I'm
a fugitive warrior to myself again
if not delusional
then at least fourth century
so I go to the bathroom
shake out my pop tarts
and build brand power
Right Guard   Trojan   Hugo Boss   Polo Blue
yes to that and we're good

7

sniff out Mick Jagger in Sunday arenas
if I fear my commanding officer
more than I fear the enemy
then advance is certain

death dipped its brush in the form for ch'i energy
that mirrored vapours rising
from cooked rice
eyes closed
will seal the lesson
of the orchard of one
and no one's infinite

earth hands us down in sleep
to serve an end
but my garden is still a desert

it says in the master's handbook
arrested development is another
albeit innocent form
of differentiation

figuration of Frank O'Hara
contemplating my father as Botero's Smoking Woman

1

Some places cough through their shoes.
Some places smoke, you listen.
White noise builds paranoia.
Mostly I'm beside myself, so
weak signals in logic is
either my place or yours

> *I came into the half-light not knowing*
> *what part of rapture*
> *stood in for reverence*

though mostly parasitized
where you come from might've been heroically decent but
so few of us roll up daggers in maps to
assassinate the head

> *from the side*
> *your ass and thighs seem to breathe in*
> *that starved museum shine*

2

I placed a rose before you and you set it down
but that's like art hung for a frame window
interrogating the unsaid
not least of which stumped me by my pins
I was swept
under the moon's lumens and learned to hunt in fog
here and not here

> *brown bronze skin*
> *and bullet nipples that remind me of*
> *the horse's tongue from* Guernica

a million chuckles
I could press my nuts to

hoard me like a criminal blinded
by greed

3

They say less is more. I wish it could cure a rainy day   *nesting*
I wish this were true of my friend Cooper who calls women food.
He calls his penis a shark. And sharks need to feed.   *your*
In all the years I've known Cooper he never talked of love   *tummy*
only of women and appetite.   *on a*
He references his heritage as less of a by-product and more of a tool.
Italian stallion. Chinese stallion   *billowing*
I say to myself. As if it were a repeatable remedy   *sheet*

4

Provisionally
the rose is a symbol to attenuate
the widely fracked *terra incognita* waiting on

astral smoke heaved out
of your stretched body appears
more sanguine than spent

my drill bit
raises its slick marmoset face

wearing the gulf   *it's early and your solid*
dispersant's calm   *cream of blowback shouldn't*
look so surfed behind those tiny ears

maybe your stoic lips should seem less fluid but
the calm I give you is given back

the best advice
is to go with flippancy
not something furry-cuddly
or worse   Buddhist

5

your voice I loved like the far end of rain
might've been engineered by a coyote
or something less mystical   a rose

now your ample display
of space would've worried
me if the gauche puffs of

a smell given greater push by city streets
maybe Mayor Nenshi's purple tie's a warning
against sock puppets for which it's always game on
when heroes slip up and lose their purple cape

footsoles
kicking lightly
hadn't conquered the
one who praised you

promising clean water after Gary Holden did Blue
Rodeo care of ENMAX to put my credit in arrears

stiffening
the oxygen dance
as only you could

let the same rains that washed the roofs at Harappa
wear slippers that cock my toes

6

to be a better predator   *I need freedom like a cloud needs wind*
the polemic insult of birth   *not knowing how*
must sex its assemblage in a soup can times infinity
since violating the sign only validates it further
pop art for its own sake   *to exceed the confines*
is a chorus with one worldview
the canonic beaver and canoe   *of an idea inside me*
making me less of a by-product and more of a tool
and what of the cost   *this giant wants out*

7

what of the cost
if lithium weren't used for air strikes
would you have given us better bowl cuts

                                                see how your eyes
                                                have already left town

and for lousy customers spilling milkshakes
on our poured UFO books
fried spit in wok grease

                                                while the towered flower
                                                on your sweet head

back-roomed calendars of Grable and Hayworth
your scrapper's alley would knock over cat trash
to get at a cigar stub
smoke-filled over Chinatown   *is as coy to surrender*
bankrolled fan-tan and bone
bed TV
land of chuckwagons   *as it is to corruption*

8

wake up, superhero sun
not going where the dark cape slides
no seed stretching
in common delight with earth
one margarita at Teatro and I'm
shitfaced   eyes
gone redundant as Frigidaire
examining my humps

out of need
to find
closure from

turning in my star
loners don't talk just to breathe do they

such permission
was never yours to grant

exclusion principle

Calgary in February

24 hours

Miss Manners

where did Metallica go?

month to month

that animal

August

Six

same love

*same elusive
love*

exclusion principle

The cosmic meadow at dusk
has no one ringing the bell to play his part.
The sky is a blue railway pushed
through with sticks of dynamite.

Dust may crumple
but the lettuce is sparkling

the foreground clangs
off this vein, this celestial
happy-go-lucky gold for faked
citizenship:

at night the town swizzles
with staked claims and letter writing.
By day the greengrocer comes
with the milk; surely
it's not the empties but the
ruminant that remains,

grove of staved vegetables
whose health in the dirt
ricochets off the prong of the grower.

Such freighted mooing gorges on
feats of reclined power
as the sky fills with dishrag soot again,
sun blade on the neck of night,
held there for the duration
of its muscle.

It's the image that lasts, while
people play out forgettably.
What sounded like dropped-fork names—
Ping, Pang, Pong—
bounding down the stairs
to the foot of the prairie
were less than rain to those who came and went.

Calgary in February

pastorally winter sucks   I see it
bouncy white and blue-tinged   but then
a hole in the Japanese lilac just for me
lets a sparrow-thing dive into its bush
dune frost pampering each blow

that'll do for comfort   a girl
with Hello Kitty western boots
daisy dress and starry leggings graphs
her mom's Kensington malt and sips
surely they're skipping like fire-eaters
toward the hurdy gurdies at Livingston & Cavell
the suavities of post-Gaddafi hipsters in
fedoras chatting up graces of the vexed
and crawly-eyed   leave it to loss
and its annealing catastrophe
to dilate their typewriters

across the street the world's
best commercials are at two
well you can put a price on just about
anyone's salted butter lavished
over the dark I'm in, thin, screamy,
and now the curtains unfold
to my astigmatism
looking out for itself

24 hours

Hotel
and a low sky's burned stamina—

      now I'm in the air. Existence
is out there

no one can speak himself when the sky
      is an unsaved language.
      Airplanes divide nothing from nothing,

me and the Belgians thinking
we saved a bit of postage on
unrequited love flung through meridians   life
in a still-warm mocha ring that didn't mean to—

that moon too.
Fleeing apology.
            Existence is out there
where trout kisses break through

existence is out there
like moths under a bright source, calm and
cognizant of this headlong drive in to
yoked *oms*, the Yoga Shala yogi next door attempting to
elevate the pre-existence on a stoop in a wife-beater watching
the midday assassin
of trains hooped for God   my crotch
inevitably smacking
its rhythms   Ceylon to Babylon Ceylon to Babylon Ceylon to

      well, that's you pretending what
you do is written big somewhere above
the hum and the doilies and the sad overhang
of insistent greys and the wrong blood donor

is existence forgotten on negative silver
by Chow Dong Hoy of Barkerville?
Spoiled eyes of excoriating politeness—
Tsilhqot'in yodeller and Secwepemc barefoot doctor
thicken like chocolate pushed from the windshield,
roaming charges on the mood of atmospheres,
trained to think the dead still have a chance in the next,
simply because
you can't take along the fluff?

Sky of stretched empties heard best
when human concentration stakes itself down
when power grids slaked on neon
elevate their cares and party hard—
when light and grief transparify each other
and morning contemplates its
impending carbohydrate   its simplicity
not yet known   to you or to me
Smoky end not completely satisfied,
I surround the ordinary not yet satisfied,
callus on my brain from pondering decades,
for this, your loose talk—

            just for you to say

                    ❖

Miss Manners

she caught me coughing in the library
named after a local librarian or researcher
or thinker or statistician-educator
whose matronly portrait still gathers reading
vibrations after all these years
the old lady looked up from her *Calgary Herald*
one last time before admonishing me to cough
into my elbow not into open air
the air her farm-dunged cracked-bellows
wheezer bags for lungs would have to process
a malingering premonition of death by
1918 Spanish Flu gasping if not drowning
in pleural fluid   fine I said   so I did
as any Ancient of Days mixing cold air
with owlless weather would harbour
sun between birds and winds
to protract the circularity of it on
those who scaffold their existence through
the actions of others who owed it to them
to be vigilant for being owed by so many
to so few   I think she spoke the Queen's English
I thought of Natalie Zina a poet who
could smell my wrist and know what
it was that I ate over the last two weeks
so it came to pass that a loud soprano could
come to deafen herself by sheer virtuosity
this old lady who smelled my sickness
counter-transferred it and helped herself
to my interiority as if it were
an emotional dyslexia she couldn't
read only ransom others for
the puff-sleeved dress she always
wanted but never got the crème
brulée stolen off her plate

where did Metallica go?

The minus-seventeen snow on Seventeenth Ave. is defeating quieter tenants
standing on proud behaviour
        purgatory west winds traffic to a standstill
      past the Chocolate Bar (never been) on Fourteenth while this
Elvira-wigged beneficence passes me as I see posters of
Fefe Dobson profoundly full-lipped her denim jacket
                           off
                            the shoulder
     mountain lake wow I'm crying to Elvira it's too late for fishnets!
and to Fefe
      as Shakira meets Penelope Cruz you can drop it! with chocolate!

Crooked sculptress, come lick a hole in my side
     your eerie stardom with its sordid sortables
       come chauffeur me your missing pumps
                    at least a riff of air to mosh
            Sisu on nuclear modernity
        care of Skepsis

if Proust crossed the line from self-realization to navel-gazing are you in any
way dire
     "medication" from the sixties
      washed down with a half Corona
                shoeshine and heavy petting
will eviscerate my take on Nirvana

here's to my wide slow   cigar   sitar
          Kandahar by Pixar
       and Sandra Dee's chinny chin chin
    the ghetto stuff'll make it new

month to month

the barista's hands are drying
while her brow dishes air that
lends such pouting
buzzwords to my head
that the PN to PZ Library of Congress depresses
the short and the long of what I've read
evoking poisonous feet

the barista's hands are drying
my awkward
Look I'm in this with you
at Pages Bookstore with an all-night vigil's glowing of the poured
animal flowerpot that
nods with no resistance
for the parts chewed off

the barista's hands are drying
foreheads   stools   clemency   and me
servicing gestures
that keep prefacing
chai cardamom latte that tenures our dailiness
I worry about the dolphin coffee
in Taiji being bled for
Rauschenberg's melancholic traffic art noise
did she call me darling late warming skyline
point is   would I believe her

one worry arrives
by locked bike and Polo Sport
hydration pack while I do February
with the usual Oakleys and brake pads if
it were up to me
its metal tips wouldn't keep loosening
due to expansion-contraction why not lie down

with the vinyl siding moaning and evening
going off like popcorn inside my pillow

the barista's hands are drying
an Old Spice flame
who will probably outlast the courtesy of my disappointment
he looks so top-heavy that if he came to bed with nothing
but a gush of nerve would she give my poem the reprieve
to ignore him by
everything but the poem the
poem she once read out loud
seduced by who wrote it
if not for his
it could've at least rhymed

a for-lease building (which used to be
the Polish Canadian Centre before it too
was killed) and some mod brick newbie
restaurant in the basement
lampshades on the main and a recluse on top
why can't the most dominant
colour of my life be me

I'm in a café called Higher Ground
down low this winter where
the fifth return gets a free
heart melt   my customer's heart
still young at fifty holding these bright
crayons in the form of waking

that animal

crying myself silly
when the barn doors of the orphanage
    closed in on my sister and me
    I became that animal
    that chews off its memory
    and limps away
like all orphanages the other
animals bite   run   return
    faces
    swallowed by an unclaimed dark
    our foster mom claimed us
    she wore a tartan that breezed
my heart to hide in
that stopped so I hid
    in tree shade near the garage
    next to the hens
    what should I have missed if it wasn't here
    to hold me
can't say
can't ask
    I'd bite others
    easily stab them
    with pencils after learning
    what it is to cry out for an other
what would
any unfinished
    monster do to find out
    how it cares
    as horribly as it learns
    to devour

❖

August

Woodwinds are carrying on
between tall necks of barley,
the original text of summer,
aphrodisiac of spring.
Responsibility to form is everything
to stillness—
as for contemplation
refiguring its frail savour
in the forest paths
sponged green with moss,
it's as if you were a magpie;
and each day is a raft
of liquid silence that
the directionless firmament
takes from its death-love grip on us.

Us because we waken to
receive each other's eyes.
Other because we're not
the same forms. When you were
Spray Lakes to my Claresholm
and you simmered me over your
mushrooms in butter, what emerged?
A blue uproar.
Too soon, the sun's feathers will measure
the highest branch of the wu-t'ung tree.
The best flute wood being
what the phoenix perched on,
it only matters that you shout
your black wings over my dead shore.

over my head

sofa

Chinese blue

a true account of the sun who
appeared to my thinking we don't
live long enough

the half-life of one

I

you're a transfigurer

on a clear day

Seven

this dance is finished
big
strutting Mao

❖

over my head

          grandiose fly   licker and barterer
of open-air digestions   of what dignified monks might call heat *cool*
                    and cold *warmth*
disjunct heaven's
          thrown out on a plague and a dime
objectivity still triumphs over it   then your lickety harelip
               flicks like Kierkegaard's
               marsupially slurpish maw

commando eulogizer of scrofulous belly hairs
     on earthly knee   to quarrel with the wind

     without prey
                                   I'm not a fly am I
                              a more squalid claim to being
                         might argue that software has no soul
                              its series of transmissions can't puzzle
                    or question its chain commands nor can it doubt whose
                    shady dialectics coerced it so Emily D. must keep
                                        cooling heaven's heels
          on such Hippocrene oaths that flutter and dither and lay

               eggs on
               tautology
               fly
               you had me at shit

even worse: reward
and punishment don't
gnaw on spiced
chicken feet neither

sludge cleaves pearls of us
thrown onto the pile
such hot envy I'd wear
black haired
wind-up vampire at the Goya heap

you remind me that
I am not my self
by Derrida alone
I'll leave you alone

morpher of sex differences
down-lit buzz bomb
doo-diddly-oodler
kimono moth of east and west

inbled by
tranquility
your history
passes gas out
the kitchen grate
no one
sutures smell
to the wind
better than you

sofa

enter the room   here she is

my sofa's restorative is resting
horizontal with the window blind and heat register
sit down
            let her weigh you down with heart advice
splendidly repressed
                        the tiptoe sufficient antimacassars
avail you a cool forearm-to-crotch meld
one more reason to stay indoors, noble one
no need to flail around a hammock's inversion
or Adirondack's open solarium to hubris
listen
        her velvet cushions so tyrannically quiet
one could sit and say nothing
as a barracuda behind glass has no
roving net to leap through   or the singular mad eye
that tries to get behind its own shadow   though clouds hum
and don't weep for apples   neither does the sofa
who respects Sun Tzu's advice that
no country has ever profited from protracted warfare
her tight buttons stick to velour
all conniving bread smell
                    plumbed and righted she's steady as a window frame
from which life parades before her
looking over the sere cliffs of Manhattan
admiring my rare nest of abacuses
beehived by bottom hair and dust bunnies coiled
about her largesse
my sofa is one lazy wonder
swallowing me by her belly lint she whispers

come to me   dream dossier
slumber rack for happy endings
my sofa watches *Mad Men*
for the same reasons I cry and measure my way to the bathroom but
my sofa fast forwards and rewinds
the secretarial coy she might role-play in *Second Life*
before sweeping me
off my feet   will we be together?
so please   sit down   relax   cigarette?
we've built a home
believe me   this siren knows no Ottoman
her gussied palm is the best seat for you
among the *hey you*s of rote and sleep

blame it on
better words

dysphoria   bad bunions
you can't force
awareness on anyone

Chinese blue

sacred wonder is a tall order
for any poem to start ending
tigers of sanctity appear
with both paws frothing

the logograph for Ten Thousand Things
resembles the sweep of a dragon
which in turn resembles a bridegroom
politicking the newly earthed

while the mere shine
of words parting the Chinese blue
cast without striking
mint their light on brazed air

a true account of the sun who appeared to my thinking we don't live long enough

it's worth it
    it's worth saying it
    to believe you'll be free if the good in weighing things can bear its
    equivocal murmur

you appeared to me one morning   naked   your crotch
    a Haida sun   each of its ten brilliant arms juggling balls that
    were simpler worlds less haunted than ours

—hey, Kroetsch! You're back! You look just like God
    in all his chi-chi filigree, like a hoarding Aztec!

Don't let the silver hair and pasty skin fool you, son, he replied, adjusting his
horn-rimmed glasses, so retro he must certainly be in Bermuda.

—so either you're dead or I'm watching you in Panavision or I'm
    dreaming …

Or none of the above, he sighed. *And don't call me God. God only looks like
what people can't see. Summer's dragonfly doesn't know what snow is, right?
Anyhow, it's all about baby steps.*

—what is? I asked.

*The way we get shown up every time we try and prove we're really here.
It's all an elaborate hoax, really. You make love, you sing a song. It's a common
song because it's just the sum of what everyone else is thinking.*

—somehow that doesn't sound very seminal, I said. You were nothing if
    not seminal.

Well, Kroetsch said, scratching his sun's balls, *at least the world's garden knows you. It's all about showing appreciation.*

—that's what I wanted to talk to you about, Kroetsch. You weren't even here long enough for—

Nobody is, kid. Don't interrupt. I'm not coming back, you know. So I'm never really gone. Got that?

—not really, I said. Like with my dad? It's different. I'm always between two things with him. What I'm seeing and what I'm imagining.

Instead of nodding, Kroetsch sucked in his gut and swung his hips back and forth. The intense Haida sun blinded me.

We can only try to be both, was all he said. *Look, you better get some rest. Stop weighing things and you'll be more likely to vanish. Good comes to those who don't overstay their welcome. Self-pity's part of the same body ache, though. And your body's all that's left of childhood. Be good to it. You just have to work out more, look at me! Whatever doesn't kill you—*

And then Kroetsch trailed off.

All of this happened on a Tuesday, July 12, 2011.

The arms of light emanating from these lines
    touched down on my forehead
    and what returned to me was an afterimage—
    thingless threads. Going. Gone.

the half-life of one

what's with the skedaddling
evening that seems
to leap down onto my chest

midnight's in me
and in a dog like you   the
dog of attachment that you are

spent of breath and ego
such recursive pause
follows me like a smell

you're the last
father of the universe
that I'd whisper to and

assail me with guilt regardless
you'd leave it to nature
not mercy

what we kept
inventing ourselves with
births wax and wane

lovers give
all they've got
then they blow apart

I

whose name do I function by
        if not my own
        words don't like to scatter

or be barren   story-stripped
        of cloud and predicate and
        abandoned by the fold

better to make me a homophone
        where *I* is an eyeful among
        slovenly beauticians

feeding brilliance
        and sycophancy
        to their caramelized epitopes

my subject self shows
        the crooked
        teeth of mere being

look, I wasn't born
        manger-style, I do snap
        and trade in salamanders' breakable substances

Aries in April
        the flowers quiver
        analects swing their genitals to no apt conclusion

persimmons if unripe will burn
    like sand around the teeth
    so what if I'm not

master of my own air
    I won't panic it
    with thoughts that bend and rise

❖

you're a transfigurer

sometimes when I'm tired I can hear my eyes blink
   at twenty-four frames per second   the analog soldier
     places a clock over his unexamined heart
               bone-dry effable heat
        is what's left of the life he had no force to think from
              after idle cylinders drained his autonomy

   events close on him
   like a krill feeder
   expels the sea from its entity
                      at twenty-four frames per second pushing
fifty
              don't I deserve to be in the loop?

As far as heaven used
      to calm me when the world defined too much,
   please don't get me wrong. My father is not my mask.
     He's the pooled sinus of failed emotive repair
       for which vision, like mismatched faith, seems to end
       on a spit with a lighthouse on it—
          you can't always define it but you'll know it when you see it—

    I'm no soldier
    smothering his chest on a kiss or a phantom pain
       one for the team
         or a ring from another planet that morning hides
        and evening detonates
    I'm awake at night and calm
bedsprings buoy me from seacoast to lunar white

     you get colder, old compasses furl, ships
     roll up the world's edge

looking out toward valleys of lives not lived
the furthest lights used to tunnel closer
when I was small
conscious of my birth
at a clear point in time far from ego—it was ego—
never meant to ease understanding it
grew alongside my own skin
that grace translated, no left or right, looking up often at
the moon's barging constancy—

Dad? Mom? Strange waves

(words again) for who I am

time
how do you empty it
or does it mean to have

surrounding me
my
name

if I take
your evidence of me
will my wandering pass

sliding off the essential sky
to say
we were here once

.

on a clear day
you can see forever

Poetry lets you hear things
poetry loosens the heart
pays it forward I mean against the world as a matter of
record when I was little
Dad's firefly
in its drifty blue cocoon of 3 a.m.
would penetrate my eyelids that I barely opened
then he would whisper
my name   *Ah-Meen, go to sleep*
a seeing layer just above my eyes
he knew I was faking sleep
the black of the cuckoo clock above his head would receive
dark heaven over the blow
of his firefly smoke throwing
meaning into shadow on the wall
the first outlined other-me I saw
to wake from   did he
also see himself
in that continuous chain of breaths of his
perhaps a reminder of the weight of home
the one he left cropless and emptied
not enough rice and the trees gnawed bare
shielded by blanket-night eyelids
its inner compost built up
and so awake I had to imagine him sleepwalking
his way up to dark heaven
here's all the time in the world to take a second
to follow and become the man who is also
self-dissolved
who must tend to the relishing
worry of starvation always a day away
but utterly free
with hunger so close by
that mere happiness

112

matters so you just take it
of thirst that matters
everything proves
its own memory so we don't lose our way
you breathe it down to your heels
the famished smoke the night
soil that this vital camphor
wisp of being still
can unburden in the next
so you grasp without taking
any grave doubt from the blind
who dream through dead eyes
and learn how nothing
flies

Acknowledgements

In my third book, *hypoderm*, Henny Penny makes a brief appearance to worry about the world's impending obliteration. To that end, the kill-or-be-killed lull got me to thinking—even as my investments tanked, even as I sat in the green glow of an electron microscope scanning a glomerulus for post-infectious subepithelial humps—what comes after the atheists and nihilists have their say? It was sheer facelessness behind the galactic-quixotic that made me stir. Well, maybe there was a star or two that winked. Suddenly the sky's tired, familiar face stared back at me, and I wanted to get to the bottom of it. So, invisibility as a place of agency began. It spoke to me from the sky over the land that fell into European laps after disease wiped out the first custodians, whose tribe names and ways are and should be a supreme compass by which all life is taught to preserve life. Here are their names:

Kainai Chipewyan Cree Heart Lake Horse Lake Bigstone Cree Enoch Cree Frog Lake Beaver Lake Athabasca Alexis Nakota Sioux Alexander Cold Lake Driftpile Duncan's Kehewin Hobbema Loon River Louis Bull Piikani Siksika Paul Montana Sawridge Mikisew Lubicon Kapawe'no Stoney Whitefish Little Red River Lake Woodland Cree Swan River Tallcree Sturgeon Lake Sucker Creek Sunchild

And there are always more unnamed than named, so I wish to thank all the spirits of those peoples for filling the sky over what us settlers call Alberta.

I have been lucky and blessed with not only the unfailing love and support of my family, but enduring friendships built over the years with those in the Calgary writing community. Here's the lowdown, in no particular order:

Sheri-D Wilson, Vivian Hansen, Sarah X. Murphy, George Melnyk, Rita Wong, Cecelia Frey, John Frey, Matt Smith, Dave Eso, Brian Kiers, Patrick Horner, David Martin, Lori D. Roadhouse, Laurie Fuhr, Irina Moga, Rona Altrows, Naomi Lewis, JoAnn McCaig, Richard Harrison, Rose Scollard, David Scollard, Simone Lee, Mark Hopkins, Kirk Miles, Kirk Ramdath, Dymphny Dronyk, Joan Crate, roadsters, hipsters, prissy perjurers, reluctant narcissists, Gung Hay Fat Choy, anyone with a bouffant.

For my family at Talonbooks—without whose professional acumen, insight and ethereal withdrawal, I might not have gone between the spaces:

Kevin and Vicki Williams, Garry Thomas Morse, Greg Gibson, Ann-Marie Metten and Les Smith.

Last but not least, to the ones who always ask, *What's up?*:

Bill Cicon, Terry Chang, Julie Sedivy, Stuart Ian McKay, Sharron Proulx-Turner.

Weyman Chan was born in Calgary, Alberta, in 1963, to immigrant parents from China. Chan wrote his first poem when he was thirteen years old. He has published poems and short stories in a wide variety of literary journals and anthologies. He won the 2002 National Magazine Awards silver prize for his poem "At work," and the 2003 Alberta Book Award for his first book of poetry, *Before a Blue Sky Moon* (Frontenac House). His second book, *Noise From the Laundry* (Talonbooks) was a finalist for the 2008 Governor General's Award for Poetry and the 2009 Acorn-Plantos Award for People's Poetry. *hypoderm* (Talonbooks), Chan's third book, was a finalist for the 2011 W. O. Mitchell Literary Prize.